Authors
*Kids Love*

# Bruce Coville

*An Author Kids Love*

*by Michelle Parker-Rock*

**Enslow Elementary**

an imprint of

**Enslow Publishers, Inc.**

40 Industrial Road
Box 398
Berkeley Heights, NJ 07922
USA

http://www.enslow.com

This book is based on a live interview with Bruce Coville on June 15–16, 2005, and includes photos from his collection.

*To all the monsters, aliens, and ghosts I have known and loved.*
*And to B.C.—thanks.*

Enslow Elementary, an imprint of Enslow Publishers, Inc.

Enslow Elementary® is a registered trademark of Enslow Publishers, Inc.

**Library of Congress Cataloging-in-Publication Data**

Parker-Rock, Michelle.
    Bruce Coville / Michelle Parker-Rock.
        p. cm. — (Authors kids love)
    "This book is based on a live interview with Bruce Coville on June 15–16, 2005"—T.p. verso.
    Includes bibliographical references and index.
    ISBN-13: 978-0-7660-2755-8
    ISBN-10: 0-7660-2755-4
    1. Coville, Bruce—Juvenile literature. 2. Authors, American—20th century—Biography—Juvenile literature.
3. Coville, Bruce—Interviews. 4. Authors, American—20th century—Interviews—Juvenile literature. 5. Children's
stories—Authorship—Juvenile literature. I. Title. II. Series.
PS3553.O873Z84 2006
813'.54—dc22
[B]

                                    2006015873

Printed in the United States of America

10 9 8 7 6 5 4 3 2 1

**To Our Readers:** We have done our best to make sure that all Internet addresses in this book were active and appropriate when we went to press. However, the author and publisher have no control over and assume no liability for the material available on those Internet sites or on other Web sites they may link to. Any comments or suggestions can be sent by e-mail to comments@enslow.com or to the address on the back cover.

**Photo Credits:** Courtesy of Bruce Coville, pp. 1, 3, 4, 6, 7, 13, 15, 20, 23, 24, 29, 30, 36, 46, 47; Library of Congress, p. 11; Michelle Parker-Rock © 2005, pp. 3, 32, 33, 41, 42, back cover.

**Cover Photo:** Courtesy of Bruce Coville.

# Contents

BOOKS

Author Bruce Coville with
some of the many books
he has written.

# Monsters, Dragons, and Ghosts

## Chapter 1

Strange things begin to happen to Nina Tanleven when she sees a ghost in the third row of the Grand Theater. Susan Simmons discovers that her substitute teacher is an alien. A toad leads Jennifer Murdley to the Beauty Parlor of Doom. Russell Crannaker's magic ring turns him into a demonlike creature. Jeremy Thatcher's orb is really a dragon's egg. An alien eats Rod Allbright's homework. Cara Hunter leaps from a bell tower and falls into a land of dragons and unicorns. Anthony and Sarah Walker encounter werewolves, vampires, mad scientists, wizards, curses, zombies, and body snatchers in Morley Manor.

What do these characters have in common? They were all created by Bruce Coville, best-selling author of books for young readers.

Many of Coville's characters and story ideas come directly from his childhood experiences. He grew up around the corner from his grandparents' dairy farm, just a few miles outside the small town of Phoenix, New York.

"Behind our house, the lawn sloped down to a swamp," said Coville.

Bruce Coville grew up outside Phoenix, New York. As a boy, he loved to play outside.

Beyond the swamp stretched a field. Beyond the field was a forest. This may sound familiar to some of my readers. It's the basis for the landscape behind Rod Allbright's home in *Aliens Ate My Homework*. Rod himself is based on me. I am Rod Allbright.

The book was illustrated by Bruce Coville's wife, Kathy Dietz Coville.

She used photographs of Coville at age eleven as references for her drawings of Rod.

Coville said:

> I'm in all my stories. If anybody reads all my books they probably know more about me than I know about myself. But Rod Allbright is consciously modeled after me. His inability to tell a lie, and the reason for it, is right out of my own life.

Many of Coville's other characters are based on the students he knew during his seven years as a teacher at Wetzel Road Elementary School in Liverpool, New York.

This class picture was taken when Bruce was in fifth grade. His wife used pictures like these when she drew the illustrations for his books about Rod Allbright.

"The kids were alive in my head," he said.

*The Monster's Ring* and *My Teacher Is an Alien* came right out of Coville's teaching experiences.

# Enchanted by Comics

As a young boy, Coville loved comic books. When a new shipment of the magazines arrived each month at his Uncle Ray's country store, Coville picked out his favorites and took them home to read. He especially liked The Amazing Spider-Man and the Fantastic Four, two of Marvel Comics' best known series. Coville's fan letters to Marvel were his first words to be printed in a nationwide publication.

Bruce Coville

The main character, Susan, in *My Teacher Is an Alien*, is a combination of all the incredible girls Coville taught.

The first version of *The Monster's Ring* was a five-page short story. When Coville started the project, he thought it was going to be a picture book called *Monster for a Day*. It was about a boy who finds a monster drawing bats on his basement wall. The creature taps the boy on the shoulder and turns him into a monster.

"The problem with the story was that the boy who turned into the monster didn't get anything out of it," said Coville. "So I wondered, what kind of a kid needs to be a monster?"

Coville looked around his classroom and found a boy who had trouble because he was being picked on.

"I took his personality and used him in the story," he said. "I based Eddie, the bully, on another kid in the same class. Duncan, the character who takes center stage in *My Teacher Fried My Brains*, is based on that same bully."

In *Into the Land of the Unicorns*, Coville tried doing something different. He created Raffaela, a girl from the *barrio*, a Spanish-speaking neighborhood.

"I didn't get very far in the story because I realized I didn't know her life," he said. "I couldn't write honestly about her. I started over again, and I put my daughter in the story instead."

Coville understands the importance of developing characters that are real and believable. He creates a character at three levels. The outer level is what others see about the character. The inner level is what the character knows about himself, such as his likes and dislikes. The third level, which Coville calls the deep secrets, is the character's desires, hopes, fears, and regrets.

Coville does not necessarily know what his characters will be like right away.

"Plot always come first," he said.

When creating a plotline, Coville often outlines the sequence of events. This helps him to know the ending of the story. Coville's plots draw the reader into his characters' lives.

Coville has many literary interests. In addition to his popular science fiction and fantasy series, he has been praised for his picture book adaptations of some of William Shakespeare's more popular works, such as *Romeo and Juliet* and *A Midsummer Night's Dream*. He also wrote four musical plays. His novel *The Dragonslayers* started out as a theater piece with songs that he wrote for his fourth-grade class. Several years later, it was performed by Syracuse Stage, a professional theater company.

Coville is the recipient of many state and national awards. There are over sixteen million copies of his books in print. He is pleased that his books have attracted so many kids into the world of reading.

"I'm a very happy guy," he said.

He is also a very busy person. "I run at ninety miles an hour for fifty weeks out of the year," he said.

When asked how he got started, Coville was quick to reply.

"Becoming a reader," he said, "was the first step."

Coville has written several books for kids based on the plays of William Shakespeare.

# A Reader and Writer

$\mathcal{B}$ruce Coville was born on May 16, 1950, in St. Joseph's Hospital in Syracuse, New York. He is the oldest child of Arthur James Coville and Jean Elizabeth Chase Coville. He and his younger siblings, Rob, Brian, and Patty, grew up in cow country in a rural community about twenty miles from Syracuse. Coville has fond memories of his grandparents' dairy farm, which was down the road from where he lived.

Coville enjoyed reading at an early age.

"Becoming a reader is the first step to becoming a writer," said Coville. "But unlike some readers who learned to read before they went to school, I did not."

He recalls three important events that had an impact on his development as a reader. The first was when he realized he could read some of the words in his schoolbook. The second was when he recognized that he was not in the top reading group. The third, however, was the most significant.

"It was when my father read to me," he said. "It is one of my most vivid memories of childhood."

Bruce Coville, age 11 months, with his mother.

Coville at age 3.

Coville's father was a devoted dad who cared about his family. However, he was a traveling salesman and was away from home a few days a week. For the young Coville, time with his father was very precious. One night, his father sat him on his lap and read to him from *Tom Swift in the City of Gold*.

> I was swept away in the story. It was important because it was my father reading to me. It was also important because I was a boy, and it made it all right for me, a boy, to read. That made me a reader.

Coville attended Cherry Street Elementary, a small school where he had many friends.

"I was with the same group of students largely from kindergarten through twelfth grade," he said. "I graduated with a class that had about a hundred people in it. They were people I really knew well."

Coville loved being a kid. He was in no hurry to become an adult.

"I was a goofy kid. When I saw *Peter Pan*, it rang instant bells for me," he said. "I was having more fun than grown-ups. They were all working, and I was having a good time. I wasn't that interested or that concerned about racing to be a grown-up."

Coville and the neighborhood kids played baseball, football, and kickball.

"I wasn't terribly good at it, but I played," he said.

Coville (on left) with his brother Robby.

He was, however, a very good student.

"My report card tended to be A, A, A, C or D. That C or D would be in handwriting. It was atrocious."

Coville disliked school only when it interfered with his life. "I had other things that I wanted to do," he said, "but school didn't bother me that much. I kind of enjoyed it."

Coville was not enthusiastic about writing until sixth grade.

"The way we learned to write was by writing to a lot of prompts," he said.

Then later in the year, something happened that made Coville believe that he wanted to be a writer.

At the end of the year, Mrs. Crandall gave us a chance to really write. She said, "We're going to write a short story. We're going to work on it every day in class, and we're going to read them all out loud." The whole thing came together because she did not tell us what we had to write. It just came from inside me. When I wrote that story, I did a really good job.

Coville thought about becoming a writer, but he thought about doing other things, too. He said:

When you're a kid you change your mind. I thought about being a doctor quite a bit, and I thought about being an actor. I love performance. In my earlier years, before sixth grade, I thought about being a cowboy, because in the 1950s, cowboys were a big thing. I didn't know you couldn't be a cowboy the way I was thinking about it. I thought about being a psychologist and an astronaut, but I kept coming back to writer.

Coville stumbled through junior high school. He did not necessarily feel that he fit in with the other students. While the other kids dreamed about becoming sports legends or fantasized about playing music in rock bands, Coville thought about writing science fiction and traveling to distant planets.

The summer between seventh and eighth grades, Coville discovered the work of author Edgar Rice Burroughs.

"He was known primarily for writing *Tarzan*," said Coville, "but what I found first and fell in love with were the John Carter of Mars books."

Carter is a hero who is transported to Mars by astral projection, which meant he could use his spiritual body to travel through space while keeping connected to his physical body on Earth.

"I really wanted to make books like that. I loved them. They drew me in. I wanted to live in that world," he said.

At about age fourteen, Coville taught himself to type.

# More Marvel

When Coville was at Duke University, he got a letter from the publicity person for Stan Lee, who was the head writer at Marvel Comics. Lee was interested in coming to the college to give a talk. Coville jumped at the opportunity. Marvel Comics had been a big part of Coville's reading diet as a boy, and as an adult, he was still a fan. Coville organized the event, met Lee, and led a lively discussion.

He said:

I got my mother's *Ten Days to Touch Typing* records. They were big black long-playing records that came with her portable typewriter. I taught myself to type so I could write. I was reading a lot of horror and dark magic at the time, and I was going to write a short story that had that theme.

In the summer between his junior and senior years of high school, Coville worked on his first novel. It started as a short story and turned into four hundred pages. Although it was not ready for publication, Coville thought the experience was fun, and he learned a lot from the process.

During Coville's senior year, the country was in turmoil. The United States had sent soldiers to help the South Vietnamese in their war against North Vietnam. Many Americans objected. Students all over the country were participating in protests against the war. In addition, African Americans were fighting for equal rights. That spring, Dr. Martin Luther King, Jr., was assassinated. Coville was extremely aware of these events.

He was chosen salutatorian of his senior class, which meant he would give a talk at graduation. Feeling emotional about the current events, Coville wrote a speech that strongly expressed his feelings. His advisor said he could not give the speech.

Coville composed another talk that was less critical about world events and more acceptable to his teacher, but when it came time to speak in front of the graduating class, Coville took a risk and presented the original speech. He wanted the audience to know what he thought and what he believed. Surprisingly, the speech he gave was well

Bruce was the oldest of four children. He is shown here (on right) with Rob, Brian, and Patty.

received. It was Coville's first experience with the power of public speaking.

After graduation, Coville left Syracuse for a summer in the Caribbean. First, he spent two weeks in New York City, where he washed dishes in a seafood restaurant and cleared tables at a cafeteria in Brooklyn while he waited for a flight to the island of St. Thomas. He spent the remainder of the summer on the island, working at the airport to earn money for college.

At the end of the summer, Coville returned to the states, ready to enter Duke University. He threw himself into college life and enrolled in a creative writing course. He also started writing letters to Katherine Dietz, a high school friend who lived around the corner from his boyhood home. At the end of his freshman year, he went back to Phoenix, New York, and took a job working at a steel mill. He dated Katherine, and he worked on his writing.

Coville said:

> She was a fabulous artist. Her mother gave me a copy of *Winnie the Pooh* to read. I loved it. I particularly loved the way the art and the text flowed together. I thought, "We could do that," because Kathy has a very whimsical style. So I thought we should try and do kids' books together. We started, and we never turned back.

# The Foolish Giant

## Chapter 3

A year after he began college, Coville left Duke University and married Kathy Dietz on October 11, 1969. Their first son, Orion, was born in 1970. The family moved to Binghamton, New York, where Coville enrolled at Harpur College, part of the state university.

"I was married, and I had a child," said Coville. "I was working a couple of jobs trying to keep food on the table while I was going to school. I knew I couldn't make a living out of writing right away."

Coville found employment in the nearby town of Owego, New York, at IBM, a company that manufactured computers. He worked at one of the stations where the machines were assembled in individual stages on a conveyor belt. He said:

> I was sitting on the assembly line at IBM, where I was doing an evening job, and I realized the smartest thing to do would be to go back to school and get my teaching degree. I could work with kids, work on my writing, and be in the right environment. I changed to the State University at Oswego. It turned out to be a very good move, because the seven years I spent teaching elementary school were part of everything I do as a writer. Books like *The Monster's Ring* and *My Teacher Is an Alien* come right out of that elementary school teaching experience.

Bruce Coville married Kathy Dietz in 1969. They had been friends since high school.

The Covilles' first child, Orion, was born in 1970.

Cara Coville was born in 1976, after the family moved back to Phoenix, New York.

Coville earned a Bachelor of Arts degree in elementary education from the State University of New York at Oswego in 1973. He and Kathy moved back to Phoenix, New York, and Coville took a job teaching second and fourth graders in Liverpool, a nearby town. The couple's second child, Cara, was born in the spring of 1975. He said:

In the summer of 1975, I took a two-week course in kids' books at Syracuse University. One night while I was babbling about the class, Kathy drew a picture and said, "Write me a story about him." It was a picture of a giant. It took a while, but I did the story.

One of the speakers at the seminar was Natalie Babbitt, the author of *Tuck Everlasting*.

"I showed her some of Kathy's illustrations. Natalie was extremely enthusiastic."

24

Babbitt suggested that Coville and his wife create a dummy, a sample book in which the text and illustrations are laid out on the appropriate pages. She told him to send it to several publishing houses. After many rejections and many revisions, they got a letter from a publisher who was interested.

"I remember the date," said Coville, "because it was 7-7-77. It was supposed to be the luckiest date of the century. It was exhilarating."

*The Foolish Giant* was published in 1978. Not long after that, Coville was driving to school when the phrase "space brat" came to his mind.

"I thought it was a hilarious idea," said Coville. "So I wrote a picture book, Kathy did some sample illustrations, and we sent it to our editor."

The editor rejected it. She did not think children would want to read about a little green being from outer space.

"So we were sitting there feeling really cranky about this," said Coville, "and Kathy said, 'Write me a story about a little boy and a unicorn.'"

## Book FACT

## Love of Reading

As a kid, Coville loved reading. He especially loved getting lost in long adventure stories.

I would read books that would make me laugh, make me cry, make me shiver with fear, and keep me awake. I wanted to make other people feel the way this made me feel.

Hugh Lofting's *Dr. Doolittle* and Eleanor Cameron's *Mushroom Planet* books were among Coville's favorites in elementary school. Lofting's and Cameron's stories had a tremendous influence on Coville's writing.

Instead, the next morning Coville wrote a story called *Sarah's Unicorn*.

I wrote about fifty drafts to get *Sarah's Unicorn* right. We sent that to the editor, and she said, "Get rid of the unicorn. Focus on the little girl and the witch. There are too many books about unicorns." And that was just dead wrong. There weren't many books about unicorns, but I could walk into the library and put my hand on a book about a little girl and a witch. So I wrote back, and I said, "You're wrong." And to her credit, she looked at it again and bought *Sarah's Unicorn*. It came out in 1979. It was our second picture book.

With the success of *The Foolish Giant* and *Sarah's Unicorn*, Coville's writing career was off to a good start. He was also very happy teaching. All the while, he was busy digging graves in the local cemetery.

# From the Grave

## Chapter 4

"It's a dirty job, but somebody's got to do it," said Coville about digging graves in Chase Cemetery.

It's not that spooky. My grandfather ran the cemetery, and I'd been running around the cemetery all my life. Basically it was a family job. Grandpa got tired of digging graves, and I got drafted to do it. I'd been mowing the grass in the cemetery for years. I knew every gravestone in that cemetery. Then I became a gravedigger. I dug graves by hand. There was no backhoe involved.

According to Coville, digging graves was not terrible work.

"It's mysterious," he said. "But if you dig the hole yourself, lie down in the bottom, see what it looks like from the bottom up, and then fill the hole in yourself, it's much less mysterious."

Digging graves gave Coville time to let his imagination wander.

"I got ideas for stories," said Coville. In his book *The Ghost Wore Gray,* two girls dig up a grave.

Coville never dug up graves with bodies in them, but his experience digging holes taught him how to write that scene.

Coville says he believes in ghosts, but did he ever see one?

This photo was taken when Coville was in junior high school. He worked in Chase Cemetery as a teenager, mowing the lawn.

"No, but I've heard one," he said, "and when I read a ghost story, I want to see a real ghost."

29

# Chase Cemetery

Chase Cemetery is located outside of Phoenix, New York. Many war veterans and members of important Phoenix families are buried there. Many of the markers are over a century old. The graves are still dug by hand.

Bruce Coville

While he was preparing for his first student production of *The Dragonslayers* in 1980, Coville's personal life was turned upside down. He and his wife decided to live apart. It was a very emotional event for the whole family. Bruce and Kathy Coville went their separate ways, but they remained friends. The following year, their third child, Adam, was born.

Coville left his job at Wetzel Road Elementary School and moved to New York City, determined to pursue his career in writing.

Bruce and Kathy Coville's third child, Adam, was born in 1981.

30

# The Book Guy

## Chapter 5

In New York, Coville focused on writing. After many revisions, *The Monster's Ring* was published in 1982. It was named a Children's Choice Book in several states. This is a unique honor because children themselves evaluate and select their favorite books for the list.

In 1984, *Sarah and the Dragon* was released. It was a sequel to *Sarah's Unicorn*. *Sarah and the Dragon* was also selected as a Children's Choice book.

Coville was pleased with his accomplishments. By that time, he had three hardcover books published by respected companies. The books received good reviews, and they sold well. Nevertheless, he soon realized how hard it was to support his family on book sales alone.

To earn more money, he wrote original paperbacks and worked for book packagers. (A packager sells an idea for a book or a series to a publisher and then hires a writer to supply the manuscript.)

As luck would have it, one of the packagers asked Coville to write a story called *My Teacher Is an Alien*. Unexpectedly, the book became an international best-seller that sold more copies in its first year than all of his other books put together. Coville followed that book with *My Teacher Fried My Brains*, *My Teacher Glows in the Dark*, and the book he is proudest of, *My Teacher Flunked the Planet*. That same year,

Bruce Coville working at his desk.

Coville jokes around with a fake brain. He doesn't really get ideas for his books this way!

the once-rejected story about the little green tantrum-throwing alien, *Space Brat*, came out and became the first in another Coville series.

Then in 1992, after eleven years of living separately, Bruce and Kathy reunited. They settled in an old brick house in Syracuse, not far from where they grew up. They share their home with

## Book FACT

# The Landmark Theater

Some sources say the Landmark Theater is haunted by an apparition, or ghost, known as the Lady in White. She often appears in the theater's upper gallery.

Some people think that she was an actress named Clare who died in the theater sometime in the 1930s. Believers say that she wears a long white gown and leaves behind a lingering scent of lilacs.

In Coville's book *The Ghost in the Third Row*, Nina Tanleven sees a real ghost. The story takes place in a theater that was inspired by the Landmark's historic setting and its resident apparition.

two cats named Dickens and Mo. Their children are grown and live close by.

Coville said:

I love this community. It's a great place to be. And it's fun for me because here I get to be the children's book guy. I've performed at the Landmark Theater, which is a grand old movie palace that I adore. We did a Halloween show there for five years with a puppet troupe. I have extraordinary opportunities in this community.

On occasion, Coville joins the Syracuse Symphony Orchestra to read his stories for live audiences.

34

Book
FACT

# Award-Winning Books

Bruce Coville's books have won many awards. Here are just a few of them:

*Aliens Ate My Homework*
Arizona Young Readers' Award
Massachusetts Children's Book Award
    (honor book)

*The Dragonslayers*
Pacific Northwest Young Reader's Choice Award

*I Was a Sixth Grade Alien*
Eleanor Cameron Award/Golden Duck Awards
    for Excellence in Children's Science Fiction
    Literature

*Jennifer Murdley's Toad*
California Young Readers' Medal
Georgia Children's Book Award
Dorothy Canfield Fisher Children's Book
    Award, Vermont

*Jeremy Thatcher, Dragon Hatcher*
Colorado Children's Book Award
Great Stone Face Children's Book Award
    (New Hampshire)
Maryland Black-Eyed Susan Book Award
Nevada Young Readers' Award
Utah Children's Book Award (Children's
    Literature Association of Utah)

*My Teacher Is an Alien*
Connecticut Nutmeg Children's
    Book Award
Children's Choice Awards in Maryland,
    Nevada, and Pennsylvania
Hawaii Nene Award

*Oddly Enough*
Best Books for Young Adults, 1995,
    American Library Association/YALSA

*The Skull of Truth*
Society of School Librarians International
    Book Award

*William Shakespeare's Twelfth Night*
Parents' Choice Silver Honor Award

Bruce and Kathy have done many other books together, including *Goblins in the Castle*, *Aliens Ate My Homework*, *The World's Worst Fairy Godmother*, and *The Mischief Monster*, the fourth book in the Moongobble and Me series.

"This is a tremendously rich time in children's books in all kinds of forms— fantasy, science fiction, historical novels, realistic and contemporary novels," said Coville. "It's a great time to be a reader."

Here is the mysterious Igor, one of the characters in Coville's book *Goblins in the Castle*.

# A Writer's Life

Chapter 6

*B*ruce Coville works in a charming old house on a tree-lined street in a residential neighborhood in Syracuse. Hardwood floors and an oak staircase give the interior an old-fashioned appearance. A stained glass window adds a whimsical touch to the first floor. The parlor is lined with shelves of Coville's books, and an adjacent room serves as the office for his business, Oddly Enough. The phone rings frequently.

Coville's own personal office is tucked away on the second floor of the house. A large desk juts out into the middle of the room. Papers, envelopes, books, and folders are piled high and cover almost

# Advice for Young Writers

Coville advises young writers to read a lot, to write a lot, to keep a journal, and to read their writing aloud. He recommends using all five senses to make a scene come alive. For example, tell the reader what a place looks like, sounds like, and smells like. Also, give characters special traits that make them memorable.

"Just keep doing it," he said. "Above all, never give up."

Bruce Coville

every inch of the surface. A computer screen glows from a nook in a corner of the room. The walls are painted forest green. On one wall there are photographs of Coville's wife and children. Awards are displayed on another. A tall wooden bookcase is stuffed with the author's books.

"I love this room," he said. "I love this computer."

Coville's life is very busy. He often works twelve to fourteen hours a day, though he does not have a regular writing routine.

"I tend to write in the middle of the night," he said. "The hardest part of writing is just sitting down to do it."

Coville also travels a great deal.

"I'm out on the road three to four months a year speaking," he said. "I don't do much writing when I'm on the road. For two weeks every year we go to a little lake in Canada called Buckshot Lake. There's no phone and no TV in the cabin. I read. I walk. We do jigsaw puzzles."

Coville said that he finds it harder to write now that he is so successful because he does not want to let his audience down. One day a month he participates in a writer's group in which the members share their writing. They offer comments to each other—both praise and criticism.

"The feedback I get is tremendously important," he said.

There are days when I feel like my brain is turning to oatmeal, and I might as well plant geraniums in my keyboard because nothing else good is going to come out of it. There are other days when I write something so wonderful that I stand up, scream, and hug myself because I can't believe how fabulous I am. But, there are a lot more oatmeal days than scream-and-hug-yourself days.

Coville said he really loves the days when enough work gets done without his being aware of it. For example, sometimes a book he is working on starts to flow on its own.

He said:

The trick is to try always to work at the top of your form. Every once in a while everything will come together, and it shoots you to another level. It doesn't happen if you wait for inspiration. If I waited for inspiration, I'd have written two stories · instead of ninety-one books.

Coville also runs Full Cast Audio, a company he founded. Full Cast Audio is devoted to publishing unabridged recordings of fine children's novels using a full cast rather than a single reader. The company has recorded the work of authors Sid Fleischman, Doug Cooney, Tamora Pierce, James Howe, Paula Danziger, and many others.

"I'm interested in virtually everything," said Coville. "It keeps life more interesting to do different things."

Coville is close to finishing the third book in the Unicorn Chronicles. The working title is *The Last*

*Hunt*, which might change by the time he finishes the book. He has plans to write a sequel to *Goblins in the Castle* and another Magic Shop book. He would also like to write more Rod Allbright books and another Nina Tanleven story.

Coville works on a recording for Full Cast Audio, which records children's books.

With so many books to his name, does he have any favorites? Coville said:

I could give different reasons to like different books. *My Teacher Is an Alien*, because it made the most money. *The Ghost Wore Gray*, because I think it's the best ending I ever wrote. I could also say *Jeremy Thatcher, Dragon Hatcher*, because if I had to guess which book would be around in twenty-five years, that's the one I'd put my money on. But if I had to choose just one book, I'd probably pick a little book called *Sarah's Unicorn*, my second book,

43

for this reason. When you start to write, you have something you're striving to create. What you have should be something better than what you were trying to do.

Coville believes he accomplished this with *Sarah's Unicorn*.

Coville also said, "I told the story that I wanted to tell in the My Teacher Is an Alien series. *My Teacher Flunked the Planet* is one of my best books and maybe the most important I've ever written."

Coville considers himself a very lucky person. He dreamed about becoming a writer, and he made his dream come true. Coville said:

Coville's license plate reads "Mr. Cranky."

Words are my tools and my toys. I love to play with words. I love creating a world, and I love creating characters kids love.

# Books by Bruce Coville

## Nina Tanleven Series
*The Ghost Wore Gray*
*The Ghost in the Big Brass Bed*
*The Ghost in the Third Row*

## My Teacher Is an Alien Series
*My Teacher Is an Alien*
*My Teacher Fried My Brains*
*My Teacher Glows in the Dark*
*My Teacher Flunked the Planet*

## Camp Haunted Hill Stories
*Some of My Best Friends Are Monsters*
*The Dinosaur That Followed
Me Home*
*How I Survived My Summer Vacation*

## Short Story Collections
*Oddly Enough*
*Odder Than Ever*
*A Glory of Unicorns* (compilation)
*Half Human* (compilation)
*The Unicorn Treasury* (compilation)
*Herds of Thunder, Manes of Gold*

## The Unicorn Chronicles
*Into the Land of the Unicorns*
*Song of the Wanderer*
*The Unicorn Chronicles*
(special edition)

## Middle Grade Novels
*The Dragonslayers*
*The Monsters of Morley Manor*
*Goblins in the Castle*
*The World's Worst Fairy Godmother*
*Monster of the Year*
*Thor's Wedding Day*

## Rod Allbright Series
*Aliens Ate My Homework*
*I Left My Sneakers in Dimension X*
*The Search for Snout*
*Aliens Stole My Body*

## Magic Shop Series
*The Monster's Ring*
*Jeremy Thatcher, Dragon Hatcher*
*Jennifer Murdley's Toad*
*The Skull of Truth*
*Juliet Dove, Queen of Love*

## Sixth Grade Alien Series
#1 *I Was a Sixth Grade Alien*
#2 *The Attack of the Two-Inch Teacher*
#3 *I Lost My Grandfather's Brain*
#4 *Peanut Butter Lover Boy*
#5 *Zombies of the Science Fair*
#6 *Don't Fry My Veeblax!*
#7 *Too Many Aliens*

43

#8 Snatched from Earth
#9 There's an Alien in My Backpack
#10 The Revolt of the Miniature Mutants
#11 There's an Alien in My Underwear
#12 Farewell to Earth

## Young Adult Books

Armageddon Summer (w/Jane Yolen)
Fortune's Journey
Chamber of Horrors: Waiting Spirits
Chamber of Horrors: Spirits and Spells
Chamber of Horrors: Eyes of the Tarot
Chamber of Horrors: Amulet of Doom
Space Station Ice-3

## Bruce Coville's Book of . . .

Bruce Coville's Book of Nightmares
Bruce Coville's Book of Nightmares II
Bruce Coville's Book of Magic
Bruce Coville's Book of Magic II
Bruce Coville's Book of Aliens
Bruce Coville's Book of Aliens II
Bruce Coville's Book of Spine Tinglers
Bruce Coville's Book of Spine Tingers II
Bruce Coville's Book of Ghosts
Bruce Coville's Book of Ghosts II
Bruce Coville's Book of Monsters
Bruce Coville's Book of Monsters II

## Space Brat

Space Brat
Space Brat 2: Blork's Evil Twin
Space Brat 3: The Wrath of Squat
Space Brat 4: Planet of the Dips
Space Brat 5: The Saber-Toothed
Poodnoobie

## Moongobble And Me

The Dragon of Doom
The Weeping Werewolf
The Evil Elves
The Mischief Monster

## Shakespeare Retellings

The Tempest
A Midsummer Night's Dream
Macbeth
Romeo and Juliet
Hamlet
Twelfth Night
The Winter's Tale

## Picture Books

My Grandfather's House
The Prince of Butterflies
The Foolish Giant
The Lapsnatcher
Sarah and the Dragon
Sarah's Unicorn
Hans Brinker

## A.I. Gang Series

Operation Sherlock
Robot Trouble
Forever Begins Tomorrow

## Nonfiction

Prehistoric People

*barrio*—A Spanish-speaking area in a city or town in the United States.

**editor**—The person in charge of helping an author get a manuscript ready to publish.

**manuscript**—An author's original text for a book.

**prompt**—A sentence, picture, or idea used as a guide to create a piece of writing.

**psychologist**—Someone who studies human behavior.

**salutatorian**—A student in a graduating class who is second highest in academic ranking. The salutatorian gives a speech at the graduation ceremony.

**seminar**—A meeting or a class on a special subject.

**subconscious**—Present in your mind without your being aware of it.

**trait**—A personal quality, such as bravery or stubbornness.

**troupe**—A group of performers who travel around.

**unabridged**—Complete; not shortened.

**whimsical**—Imaginative, fanciful, amusing.

Graham, Paula W. *Speaking of Journals: Children's Book Writers Talk About Their Diaries, Notebooks, and Sketchbooks.* Honesdale, Pa.: Boyds Mills Press, 1999.

Marcovitz, Hal. *Bruce Coville.* Philadelphia: Chelsea House, 2006.

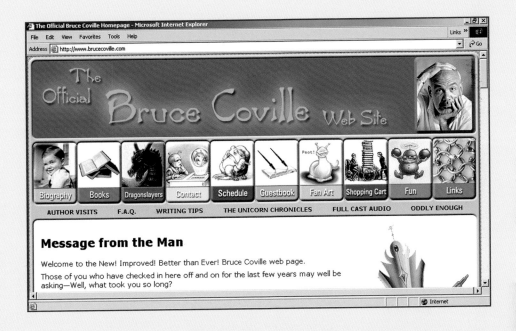

## The Official Bruce Coville Site
<http://www.brucecoville.com>

## Full Cast Audio
<http://www.fullcastaudio.com>

## The Unicorn Chronicles
<http://www.unicornchronicles.com>

# Index